DESIRE:

How do you want to feel?

chad prevost

The Big Self School is a learning community whose central mission is to help change-makers and visionaries deepen their self-awareness and relationship so they can sustainably impact the world. We create digital courses, online community, books, and media designed to activate self-awareness, deeper connections, bold action, and healthy habits so you can play big without burning out.

www.bigselfschool.com

Printed in the United States of America

Text layout and design: Averil Eagle Brannen

Library-of-Congress Control Number is available upon request.

ISBN: 978-1-945064-24-1

eISBN: 978-1-945064-25-8

OTHER BOOKS FROM THE BIG SELF SCHOOL:

DESIRE:
How Do You Want to Feel?

THREE

FOREWORD

WE HELP PEOPLE TO BE THEMSELVES.

We help people to be themselves. Sounds simple enough, doesn't it? On the one hand, it's true. There is great simplicity and insight into finally realizing that all social reformation and revelation begins with the individual. The harder part is discovering authentic principles and living by them day by day, moment by moment.

One of the most fascinating things about this work is discovering for ourselves that there is no defining characteristic of those who have found themselves. What do we mean "found themselves"? We mean you were born who you needed to be. You possess gifts and a unique constellation of atoms and neurons all firing to make you already whole. You have to inhabit that wholeness. You have to settle into it. You know it when you are there, and yes there is a "there." Your pursuits may be never ending, just like you have to exercise to remain in shape, but you can also achieve a level of emotional fitness that feels great and is sustainable. In other words, just because the process is cyclical doesn't mean you never arrive at your promised land.

Finding your way to your desire requires a number of the principles we teach at the Big Self School. It requires a calm center and, paradoxically, the courage to put the ideas into practice. Whether you think you know your desires, but want to reconnect to them, or you simply have no idea, this book can help you realize your way to a deeper and more authentic connection with yourself and what you truly want.

ONE

What feelings, experiences, and values do you want to live with?

For many, desire is a four-letter word. It's a cliche in a rock song that all-too-conveniently rhymes with fire. U2's Bono says this about their song "Desire":

Sometimes, I come across as if I got into U2 to save the world, whereas I got into U2 to save my own ass. 'Desire' is my way out. In Downtown LA, South Central LA, the people have different ways out. The crack dealers, that's their escape...I'm not passing judgment. It's their only way out. I've found mine. I'm singing about sex!

That's just it: desire leads you out. Paying attention to your longing — whatever name you give it — leads you to life. Desire is there even if you aren't sure where it went or how in the world you will access it again. Desire may go dormant as you play all the ready-made roles that adulthood throws at you, but it's there even in dormancy, steady as a heartbeat, ready to be resuscitated.

And even Paul David Hewson (aka Bono) would tell you, you have to keep your desire tuned. Keep in touch with your desire and it will keep you tuned up and tuned in.

You may not even think right now you really want it. Desire, your deep longing, what makes you feel really good just to think about, that kind of desire maybe doesn't even fit in the status quo, or at least the standards and expectations of your loved ones. You may not be ready to break out. The status quo exists for a reason, right?

That's resistance talking. Can you hear it?

It's comfortable in the status quo. Sure, there are the small gripes, frustrations, the petty grievances we all feel, but there's a certain pragmatism, an easy, reasonable guidance of following the patterns that are there (versus the uninhabitable or unimaginable ones) that aren't.

We all know there is no such thing as Utopia. There is no perfect place. That's half the definition of Utopia: a perfect place that doesn't exist.

Honestly, high achievers can be really bad about this part. You have more or less figured out how to play the game by following rules and expectations. You don't like activities with unclear outcomes like brainstorming and assignments with multiple options. Being told what to do is safe even if not always exciting, and safe is something. Safe can hold you down for a while. This is nothing against making A's. You're supposed to do what your teachers instructed. You learned, you even succeeded.

If you're here, you may well be in a vulnerable stage of life, or perhaps just buried in monotony. You know something isn't right. You know you don't know something, and you hear people talking about what they do know with conviction and it sounds nice like maybe there's something you really are missing out on.

So, hard truth number one: the truest path to finding your desire is through self-confrontation. You've got to strip that mask off.

Still with me?

Don't worry, the idea is to have plenty of radical self-compassion as well. The main goal of finding your desire is to help you live out a life in tune with what energizes you, to help you rejoin your soul and your role. The role part can be the trickiest of all. How can we really be fulfilled in a job in supply chain management when we want to be carving up the slopes in Breckenridge, Colorado? First, finding your desire is larger than how it aligns with your vocation, but as making a living makes up a considerable part of how we spend our time, that can be one of the biggest questions of all.

So yes, you do need to take an active role and do some real listening. The good news is there are shortcuts (so to speak) to our self-understanding — and where our desires rest. Desire is ultimately about how you want your feelings, experiences, and values to line up in your life.

Feelings are a great guide. No, you shouldn't always or only "trust your gut," but if you're tuning in, they are speaking. And probably too they are all over the place, and you should listen to them all. There are core emotions: anger, sadness, happiness, and fear, but there are hundreds of positive and negative feelings. More on feelings shortly.

Experiences don't just mean peak experiences like the time you mountain-biked Moab or swam across the English Channel. There are experiences of love and intimacy. Experiences of going to ballparks, taking walks in the woods, filing reports, meeting deadlines, buying or selling material things, listening or playing music, eating good food with friends, going to poetry readings, lifting weights, intermittent fasting, attending communal functions, laying concrete, making beer, opening a store, quilting. I could go on.

The question is what are the experiences you want to make happen in your life? What do you want to do bucket-list-wise, and what do you want to build into your life on a seasonal, monthly, weekly, or daily basis?

But what if your values aren't all that clear to you in the first place? Let's conclude this section with an informal exercise.

Step 1:

Choose your top value from each of the five value lists below.

Abundance Acceptance Accountability Achievement Advancement Adventure Advocacy Ambition Appreciation Attractiveness Autonomy Balance Being the Best Benevolence Boldness Brilliance Calmness Caring Challenge Charity Cheerfulness Cleverness Community Commitment Compassion

TOP VALUE: _____

Cooperation Collaboration Consistency Contribution Creativity Credibility Curiosity Daring Decisiveness Dedication Dependability Diversity Empathy Encouragement Enthusiasm Ethics Excellence Expressiveness Fairness Family Friendships Flexibility Freedom Fun Generosity Grace Growth

TOP VALUE: _____

Flexibility Happiness Health Honesty Humility Humor Inclusiveness Independence Individuality Innovation Inspiration Intelligence Intuition Joy Kindness Knowledge Leadership Learning Love Loyalty Making a Difference Mindfulness Motivation Optimism Open-Mindedness Originality

TOP VALUE:_____

Passion Performance Personal Development Proactive Professionalism Quality Recognition Risk-Taking Safety Security Service Spirituality Stability Peace Perfection Playfulness Popularity Power Preparedness Proactivity Professionalism Punctuality Recognition Relationships Reliability

TOP VALUE:_____

Resilience Resourcefulness Responsibility Responsiveness Security Self-Control Selflessness Simplicity Stability Success Teamwork Thankfulness Thoughtfulness Traditionalism Trustworthiness Understanding Uniqueness Usefulness Versatility Vision Warmth Wealth Well-Being Wisdom

TOP VALUE:_____

Step 2:
Arrange your values in the order of most important to least.

Is this an accurate representation of who you are in terms of your values?

Step 3:
Pick a wildcard value out of the entire list that didn't make the final cut. Place it in your top 5. Which one gets bumped out?

Are there values that are in conflict with one another?

Step 4:
Rate each of your top 5 values on a scale of 1-10 in terms of how much you live each one out.

What values do you live out and what values are suppressed?

Change is guaranteed one way or another

I get it. If you don't know what you want in the first place how are you supposed to pursue it? Well, you do both. You pursue knowing it, and you pursue it when you know it.

Your desire is likely not one thing, and it probably won't stay the same — although there are a few exceptions to both. Let's dig a little deeper on this. If you only have one desire and that desire is perfectly static because you're so obsessed with your desire, then you probably already know it. You don't need this book. Things are clear and definitive. You have an obsession. That's your story, and you're sticking to it.

Most people are not like that. Psychologist Dan Gilbert has even conducted some pretty popular studies to prove it. He calls it "the end of history illusion." No matter our life stage, from young to old, we have a bias toward the past. We are better able to recognize how much we've changed from the past than we are able to recognize how much we will change in the future. We are works in progress that believe we are already fully formed.

Gilbert's team measured the preferences, values, and personalities of more than 19,000 adults between the ages of 18 and

68. They were asked either to predict or reflect. The predictors were asked how much they would change over the next decade, and the reflectors were asked how much they had changed in the past decade. The reflectors realized that even qualities they had once felt were unchangeable had in fact changed immensely. Even core values related to pleasure, honesty, success, and security had metamorphosed.

Almost no one knows what they want to be when they grow up at an early age. And when you do it comes with a lot of trial and error. It is a rare exception if someone knows what they want to do, is super great at it, and has all their dreams come true at an early age (looking at you, Taylor Swift). The truth is, the vast majority of us are floundering and confused.

So what is your desire? Maybe that's the wrong question to lead with.

Besides death and taxes about the only other thing you can be certain will happen is change itself. The personality forms between the ages of five and six, but because of a concept called plasticity, it continues to adapt and change. While your core personality remains intact, the truth is through life experience, you will change. You will change as an individual, and the generation of people that will age along with you (your peers) will also collectively change.

The biggest changes occur between age 18 and your late 20s. It's not necessarily your core personality that is changing, but your values, your commitments, your tastes. These things are likely to change. Does it make sense that we're expected to make lifelong commitments to another person, as well as what we're going to do with the rest of our life before most of our personalities have even formed?

The truth is you have many selves with many possible lives with you. Walt Whitman wrote: "Do I contradict myself? / Very well then I contradict myself; / (I am large, I contain multitudes)." He meant it in the democratic sense that we all contain many selves, and we are all very much alike. It can be exhilarating to imagine all you want to do and to get in touch with the longing hidden within each possibility. Then, you are met with one huge qualifier: You will never be able to live them all out.

We have powerful imaginations and fantasies. We can see the challenges and rewards in living out any number of ways, and it doesn't seem fair that we don't get to try them all out. We do have to make choices because our time is finite. We'll get to realities like time and money further on, but for now consider two things: (1) your choices are important and beautiful for the very reason that there is something at stake; and (2) change is guaranteed. How do you want to navigate and guide the changes that will inevitably keep coming?

Pursue it through the initial resistance

Now you get to think about what is happening within you right now that sounds like a plan. You get to figure out what you are going to do with your "self" such as you find yourself right now.

Hopefully, if you've come this far you are pursuing it — you're at least a little curious, you're putting your toe in the water, you're like DaVinci's Adam holding your finger out to the Almighty with curiosity but also maybe a little reluctance. This book is ready to help you move mountains. The mountains are big and they have been inside you a long time and possibly you believe they aren't going anywhere. The mountains are obstacles, and, sure, it can be inspiring to learn about all the people that decided the obstacle was the way, but in the end, an obstacle is an obstacle.

There are these things called commitments, right? You may have commitments to other people that conflict with your desire. There is also this thing called money. There are kids possibly, or others to think about, not just yourself. There's a reason you've barely got time to finish this paragraph while eating a snack between appointments and obligations.

But you have to pursue the pursuit, you have to be curious about what you're going to learn. Knock and the door really does open. Look, it's your one lifespan which contains multitudes. All the people who have died and are suffering right now in our current pandemic are proof that the future isn't guaranteed.

Have a little fun. Experiment with yourself.

Do you want to live out your own desires, or live for someone else's?

Think of yourself as starting out on a quest and you don't even know what the quest is. You do have one. The first quest is to quest into yourself and find out what makes you feel good.

What lines up with your values? What makes you feel good?

These are the questions you should keep returning to on your quest right now. Decide it is your time. Pursue it.

You're discontented but you don't know what you can do about it

The truth is people who get what they want tend to be the ones who make the effort to know what they want. In our book, *What Do You Expect?: Discovering Methods for Deep Calm*, we discuss the nature of anger and where it comes from. Anger comes from a feeling of discontent and disrespect. It's natural and normal to feel it, but the great philosophers advise us to keep it out of our actions. It is the most "savage" of emotions, argues Seneca. In cases of sustained and collective oppression against a people group, certainly, there is a place for justified outrage.

Another form of anger turns into depression when we turn the anger inward at ourselves and/or we are denied the expression of our anger to the ones close to us. If you are inured to anger or depression, even if it's burning at a low-grade temperature, then desire may feel a long way off.

We turn to anger at others and ourselves when things aren't going according to our expectations — and when we feel out of control. At the time of this writing, the collective anger in the United States is soaring. We're in the middle of a global pandemic and that fact alone creates tension from all sides. We can't get mad at the virus, but we can get mad that we have to wear masks, or that others want us to wear masks, or that others aren't wearing masks.

Complaining about our situations is as common as the rain. Whenever we're a part of a system, even if that system is something we choose to participate in or not, we find fault. When I was in seminary, we complained about the curriculum. We complained about the lack of leadership from women and minority voices, about the lack of speaking out against injustice. In my creative writing graduate studies, we complained about the lack of community and the lack of guidance from our professors in the program.

Every institution I have worked at, colleges, universities, and startups, has had its share of outraged complainers. When my wife went to work in the sharky, tech-startup world as a community leader and then as a CEO, and I shifted into a role of a domestic dad, we had no idea how powerful and deeply embedded the forces of sexism resonate. We had no idea what would come up within each of us personally and in our marriage.

For years on end, it was almost a nightly occurrence to complain about the issues she dealt with in the workplace. Complaining is easy, even fun, compared with the challenge of creating a plan for positive change. That's just it. When it comes to doing something about the complaining, a funny thing always happens: We run out of things to say.

I understand the buzzkill. Watching some of the brightest people I've ever met struggle to invent practical alternatives to sexism and racism, I gained a huge respect for anyone who pushes beyond bellyaching and into clarity.

First, let's clarify something: there are more or less two kinds of problems. There are what Bill Burnett and Dave Evans call "gravity problems," and there are problems that you can stand to do something about. If you wish you weren't bound to the earth, or that at least it would be easy to hike up a mountain, you've got a problem that's going to be hard to get around. There's this thing called gravity.

Gravity problems are similar to life reality problems. Teachers generally don't get paid much. Doctors have to go to school for a decade or more. People who are innocent are jailed. Oppression exists. We are harming the planet with our pollution.

The best thing to do in the face of stubborn types of problems is to practice a calm mindset. You must learn to accept certain realities. It's not that you shouldn't pursue a life dedicated to earnest work on fighting a system that you believe should change. In fact, we think you should. For the purposes of this book, we want you to find your desire, and in order to do that, you have to start with where you are right now, grounded in reality. That's where you begin to design ways to your desire.

We see clients and students complain in rich detail about the things that are wrong: no one listens, their husbands or bosses are overbearing, the education system is terrible, their kids won't do their homework without handholding, their artwork won't sell.

When it comes to doing something about the things we're always complaining about, people speak in generalities. "I just want love," they say.

"Passion."

"Inner peace."

"Freedom."

It's like telling your designer, "I don't know what I want. Just make it cool. I'll know it when I see it." I've actually seen CEOs do this firsthand. It's maddening to the designer. And you are literally the designer of your life. It's time to get specific.

Another thing we hear a lot are people stating what they want, but then never doing almost anything to follow through. You say you want to travel more, but you never even look at where you'd like to go or when you'd like to be there. You say you want your kids to listen to you, but you never work on parenting methods to understand your child.

Here are your takeaways from this chapter:
(1) Make a commitment to bettering yourself by clarifying your desires.

(2) Be prepared for the action steps to make it happen once you do.

Did you lose it along the way?

It would be a tad facile to state point-blank that you once had your desire — whether or not you knew it — and now it's all about re-finding it. Some theorists advise that in fact we are all complete originals and that who we are is already complete within us from the very start, much like the acorn that becomes the mighty oak. They would have us be reminded of who we are. James Hillman, author of *The Soul's Code* is one such thinker.

Others long for the mystery and magic of a certain period in their childhood when it seemed they were most in tune with who they were. Most can identify a time somewhere between age five, as language and a more complete sense of "self" has emerged, and the pre-teen years, when one was still immersed in childhood but with twice the life experience of the young child. It might be worth some reflection to consider memories that stand out, and what they might tell you about who you were from an early age.

The explosive changes of teenaging usually tell another story. The early teens are such a baffling and strange time for our identities because of the role others place in our self-perceptions, the power of peers and those who were outside our tribe become so important. Also because the claims of adulthood are latching, and life becomes less mysterious and filled with vague but serious expectations on becoming something.

Dan Price, author of *The Moonlight Chronicles*, and self-described "hobo artist," has created a compelling example of following his way back to what it felt like as an 11 and 12-year-old when it comes to his simple way of life in the Oregon hills, living on less than $5,000 a year. It appears to be a deeply fulfilling life. Certainly, there are parts to how he lives that our larger culture should hear. We should waste less. Less is more.

He has also created what many would describe as a dream life. Not only that but in the spirit of the individual self to find freedom and pursue happiness, has he not embodied that vision?

I would get lonely, but he looks fulfilled. We're all on a different path of finding what fulfillment means to us, and I have massive respect for those who consciously live it out in their own life.

No one other than you can say whether or not you ever "had" desire in the palm of your hand at some pristine moment in your life. That is more the subject matter for knowing who you are and building self-knowledge. But we discuss it here for the purpose that pursuing your desire is about listening to your self. Listen to what yourself is telling you (or has told you at other times in your life). We trace that primarily by following feelings both good and bad.

Desire has a way of emerging within you like a secret. It ripens within your body like a seed in some remote pasture planted long ago. Over some vast distance, it has grown within you, even without you knowing it. It leads you to an intimate relationship, to a personal transformation, to the life you want for yourself. Desire isn't all sunlight and peaches, either. It can be dangerous out there, setting yourself free. If you follow your inner desire to where it meets the edge of the outer world, you may be taking a risk. That is a part of it. You cannot let yourself be denied, and the truth is, if you've really found your desire, you won't let yourself be denied. You will have found a purpose that enlarges and enriches your life, and you will be willing to sacrifice for it.

Start where you are

We should acknowledge right here and now that you are also dealing with very real constraints. Those have to be dealt with in your decisions as you pursue desire.

The high-achiever student in you wants a specific format. Be patient with yourself as you access your longing. It is a process, but I promise, if you knock with persistence, the door will open. And isn't it nice to know there isn't a prescribed formula? People and institutions have been selling you formulas all your life. Marketers and TV commercials have their formulas for influencing what you desire.

As for prescriptions, think about how effective personality tests are in helping you find your desire. Not very. For all of the ways in which humankind has addressed the idea of specialization and "what you should do with your life," we have done little to address how you should know.

I love the Myers-Briggs as much as anyone, but first, it's a simple test invented the better part of a century ago. I took batteries of Myers-Briggs constructed tests pre-enrolling into seminary. They told me this was to help me know if the ministry was "really" for me. I remember feeling vaguely threatened.

Would I take the test in a way that would reveal I was cut out to be something I didn't want to commit the rest of my life to?

Do these tests really help with important things like discovering your identity through your desire? Sure, you might learn that an INFP (introverted, intuitive, feeling, perceptive), might go into teaching and counseling and writing. At the same time, the pairings of what we might be good at might be odd or incongruent: "You indicate a facility with numbers and an inclination to work with animals."

Let's keep telling it like it is. It is frightening just how alone we are in the task of discovering our desire.

Name it and claim it. When you look desire in the eye big things begin to happen. You get closer to your reality — starting where you are. Start with what you are grateful for. Soon, you will see a way forward.

For all that you are grateful for, what isn't lining up with your values or experiences?

Desire at an early age doesn't mean anything now

There have been many interesting studies on the subject of identity and whether or not some version of your early self may be the source of your desire. Some have shown that early interest in a possible job-related skill is not necessarily useful. The neighbor's kid who jumped his tricycle over sidewalk steps continued jumping and became a competitor with any machine that involved jumping from skiing to skateboarding to motorcycles. It was the thrill of the actual "jumping" not the events or competition or winning that kept him involved. He became an electrician.

Often, the early attraction is the experience rather than the outcome or product, which, yes, can be a desire you may want to pursue, but at the same time not one to be associated with vocation. Perhaps you enjoyed flying as a child. That doesn't mean you become a pilot. You liked cooking, but maybe you won't like being a sushi chef. Maybe you like speed, but not racing. Maybe you like writing poems but not developing a publishing career out of it. A child's interests do not depend on a good product, and that is what you might have found liberating in those early pursuits or expressions.

In some respects, it should be refreshing that if you haven't found your "thing" at an early age you didn't miss out on half your life. It means you're like most people. The 2010s popularized a lot of literature that in order to be an expert at something you had to put in your 10,000+ hours of concentrated attention on a single activity, and this probably had to be achieved at a prime early age because the windows of opportunity get smaller as you hit adulthood, the obstacles multiply. Now, a new round of literature celebrates the generalists, those who have tried many things and are well-rounded and can fit their skills into a number of possible directions.

Obsession has its place, but generalists find other ways to develop their skills and careers with a broader range of interests and different kinds of creativity rather than a specific focus. The studies and experiences also tend to show that, in the end, the generalists may get to the same level of expertise as the super-focused ones, but because the paths to get there were broader, those with "range" could be more resilient when faced with challenges or resistance.

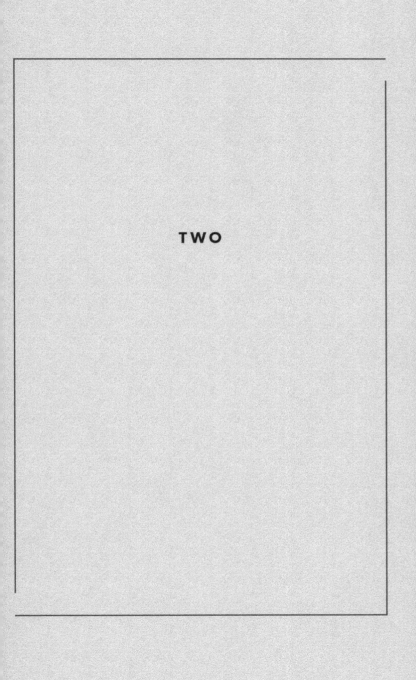

TWO

Why do some know their thing so well?

But you have so much pent up inside you, just waiting to be released, right? All around you are examples of artists and doers and thinkers and makers who have found their singular creative pursuit. What if lots of things ring your bell and you're just not sure what to focus on? So many of the stories we hear about are the successful, crazy, wild, innovators who seem to be driven to do their "thing," whatever it may be, above all else. Sometimes they may share their struggle, a setback, an obstacle, a moment of uncertainty or loss, but none ever seemed to question what they're supposed to be doing. Even when they say their process or experiences are impossibly hard, they stick with it, they grind, they do it anyway — because they feel they need to.

Does your life's passion, your "thing," ever make itself known to you? Does it come through the pursuit of self-knowledge and desire? Or do you just choose something you like and commit to it wholeheartedly? How do you know what your be-all and end-all is? If you meet big resistance, do you fight through because that's all a part of the life struggle, or do you take it as needing to "fail fast" and redirect? If you have asked questions like these you are in very good company. It may even be part of your process. Sometimes you flounder, you cast about. Then, you bring it into consciousness. You start asking questions.

Maybe it's not even that you've never nailed your exact thing, maybe you have spent loads of time on something but you've never directed your energies with purpose. Maybe you've put in your 10,000 hours on the guitar, but maybe you didn't always know why you were memorizing patterns and chords. Maybe you were finding yourself all those years and weren't paying much attention to your desire. Lots of people practice at things that might be their desire, but for any number of reasons, it never translates to getting outside their room.

What if you dream of becoming a writer, of writing that great novel? You don't know exactly what it would be about, but still you keep writing. You've got documents with big ideas scattered throughout your DropBox files with hundreds of thousands of word counts and thought trains and experiments. You've even got journals with handwritten lessons and quotes and habits tracked and measured. You catalog articles, you make plans, but you never do anything with them. Maybe you see it as a private form of self-improvement. Whatever the reasons, sharing your ideas with others enervates you. Meanwhile, all around you, everyone seems to be contributing, writing books, sending out newsletters, making YouTube videos, and starting online businesses.

Wanting to throw yourself into grand, meaningful, generative work, but not knowing what it is or how you should decide to take action is also a common human experience. We empathize. Feeling discouraged is part of the process too. And it may be something that gets incorporated into the work. Being discouraged is a universal human experience. Negative feelings give you feedback too.

We don't want to hear from the award-winning novelist who Tweets that she's only written 200 words that day. That person knows her thing, and she is good at it, and even if she's struggling at least she's struggling with writing.

So, what do we do with the questions? Where are you at?

Very likely as you take some personal inventory, you're going to become aware of your mistakes, your false steps, all the choices you made or that were made for you, that led you to right here. It's fair to give yourself a clear-minded assessment, but too much self-judgment doesn't yield the confidence-building results you need, either.

Begin with a little compassion for yourself. Be gentle. Don't dwell on what you could've, should've, would've done. Dwell instead on where you want to be, the kind of life that sounds fulfilling, fantastic, exhilarating.

How do you do that? That's all a part of what the rest of this book is about. Sometimes, we get in our way through lack of confidence or lack of clarity. That's where the magic of hunting down your desire manifests. It helps you burst through the fog with courage and purpose.

At the early stages of your endeavor to find your desire you should input more than output. Keep asking questions. How do people really make their desires happen? Read, watch, look, and listen.

Building your why

German philosopher Frederick Nietzsche once said, "He who has a why can endure any how." Knowing your why is an important first step in figuring out how to connect to your desire, and ultimately connect it to what you do. Who you are should integrate with what you do. Only when you know your why will you find the courage to take the risks needed to get ahead, stay motivated when resistance emerges, and move your life onto an entirely new, more challenging, and more rewarding trajectory.

Figure out the reasons why you must follow through with your respective goal and cannot live without it. These reasons will help you develop your drive towards your goal and make you pursue it with all your might. As civil rights leader Howard Thurman once wrote, "Don't ask yourself what the world needs; ask yourself what makes you come alive, then go do that. Because what the world needs is people who have come alive."

Desire comes from the heart over the head. Desire is a longing within you for something that seems out of reach. Like John Cougar Mellencamp's song, "Come on baby, make it hurt so good / Sometimes love don't feel like it should / You make it hurt so good." It hurts to feel what it would be like to possess the life you want to manifest, so possibly you avoid it. Let it be your guide. Envision what you want, and when it begins to hurt with how bad you want it, that is giving you information.

What is it that you are missing out on right now? How does that make you feel about yourself and your life? Write it down. Track your thoughts. If you could say in one word what you want more of in life, what would that be?

When it comes to discovering your inner why, we hear a lot of people in our community and in our workshops say their biggest struggle is that they don't know what they want to do. They want more clarity on figuring it out. A great many say they want freedom. Many also name joy. We hear a lot about wanting more balance.

We all want freedom, yet so many people are resistant to doing what's required to get it. We want to feel free, yet are scared to do what's necessary to become free. It might take courage, or it might come from taking small actions over time, voting on behalf of yourself. No single instance will transform you, but as the votes build up, so does the evidence of your identity. It requires following your authentic values and beliefs, and building strong boundaries to protect yourself from what others will tell you is right for you or try to force on you.

What you focused on in the past has made the person you are now. And what you focus on from this moment forward shapes the person you'll become. Remember that as you read this book, and consider your approach.

Forge your own path in life and work, despite resistance. Take obstacles as personal challenges to move through. Be your own highest authority on life and work. The hard part is learning that means you are responsible for your own freedom. We live in extremely unusual times right now. People are freeing themselves from various tyrannies all over the United States and throughout the world. It's time to speak out and speak up. Don't let employers or others keep you from thinking your own thoughts, and taking your own bold, unique actions.

Let's admit also that this isn't easy. It's a process.

Dreams and expectations

A funny thing happened on the way to the Enlightenment. Through more access to published material, to the evolution of the vocation myth (that you should know what you're going to do in a short amount of time and for the rest of your life), to other social and cultural forces, we began to see a job as something that connected to who we are. We came to believe that our jobs should define our identity, at least in part.

On the one hand, this is good in many respects, especially when it comes to individual and personal freedom. This is about being able to follow "who you truly are" and find fulfillment. Who wants to be a baker or a cobbler or a farmer just because it's what was expected of them all along and their ancestors had all done the same thing? Well, for some it may come as a comfort, and perhaps when opportunities were scarce, both with jobs as well as education, it was nice to know what you would do to provide for yourself and family.

Now, all you have to do is educate yourself, dream a big dream, work hard and eventually you'll find what you were born to do. Then comes the problem of flawed systems that themselves don't achieve the ideals of a just society. Not everyone has access to the same quality of education. The truth is also that there simply isn't an endless source of opportunities. At the same time, the modern world promises us that we all have limitless potential to succeed.

How many self-help books tell us that with a good use of our time and very little money all that's really required is the will to follow through and a positive attitude? Just look to the high platform achievers on Twitter and find all the *New York Times* bestsellers and Medium bloggers telling you how you too can become a success like them. This story we collectively believe, that merit finds its reward, is not going to come true for all of us even if we follow all the directions on the back of the box. There is a reason these people are in positions of prestige and power: it's not there for everyone. In fact, only a very few will succeed.

Where does this leave the rest of us who were dreaming big dreams? How do we go about the rest of our lives realizing at some point we missed the bus? If you failed to realize an earlier version of yourself, you are the rule, not the exception. To make things worse, as the story goes, it is your fault you failed.

Why "others" are unreliable and why you still need them

In the months leading up to graduation from Baylor University as an English Major I had no idea what I wanted to do or what I should do. There wasn't any clear path like there is for some professions. At the same time, I was only just getting comfortable in Waco. I had transferred there my junior year. I had a girlfriend. On top of everything else, it had taken me a long time to become a serious student. Now that I finally realized learning was a privilege, and that the life of a student was really wonderful, I had to stop and enter the great unknown of the "workforce"?

My dad was a minister and my mom was a middle school English teacher. I had no professional connections. I wanted to be a writer but had absolutely no idea how to go about it.

When I learned that a brand new seminary was being founded, I figured why not apply? One of the things I wanted most to learn in the process of deciding whether or not to go to seminary was the same question I wanted to learn once I began seminary: How do you know what you are supposed to do? Other ways this was put through texts and assignments and lectures and batteries of personality tests was: What is your calling? What is God's will for your life? and so forth.

Ultimately of course there was no answer, no clear answer anyway. Everyone wants that "burning bush" experience (or many say they do), in which Moses was told what he was to do. Or like Augustine who went through a definitive career change. As he tells it, he went for a walk one day in Milan and heard a child singing a beautiful song that he didn't recognize. The song's chorus was "pick it up, pick it up." Although he was a pagan professor of literature at the time, Augustine took the words as a command from God. He was to pick up the Bible, and read the first words he set his eyes on. The message told him to change his life. Clear orders from above.

One of the "answers" during the first year in seminary that I found particularly irritating about how you can know what you're supposed to do (or what God's call for your life is), was that we know who we are from what others tell us. That surely wasn't the transcendent message I was hoping for.

There are lots of reasons not to do what others tell us. One gigantic reason is that many people — even (or especially) those who are close to us — have agendas for us. They want to see us become something for how it would reflect on them, or possibly what they could get out of it. Not that it's always so Machiavellian. Probably as often as not, it's unconscious. Also, people know as much about you from what you reveal and how you represent yourself as by what they observe you doing. In other words, through your own lack of self-knowledge you may misrepresent yourself authentically. The point is, few people "know" us so well as to be reliable guides on how to choose incredibly important things like what we are going to do with our lives.

Frederick Buechner wrote one of the most widely quoted formulations of vocation among contemporary Christians. "The place God calls you to is the place where your deep gladness and the world's deep hunger meet." Between that statement and Joseph Campbell's even more famous, "Follow your bliss," for a little while I thought I had begun to figure it out.

But what does Buechner mean by "deep gladness"? Does he mean desire? Does he mean contentment? Does he mean the kind of joy that can be present even in the midst of suffering? And what does Campbell mean by bliss? Does he mean desire? Or does he mean passion? Does he mean contentment? And what is the difference?

With all of that said, it is understood both from philosophical and psychological traditions that you are not going to ideate your way to complete self-knowledge or only feel your way to desire. Developing an integrated self-knowledge does not happen "in a vacuum" as they say. There are no perfectly reliable guides, and others will have to do.

Desire and luck

Besides how others contribute, finding your desire may also require a different theological construct: blind dumb luck. We can call it serendipity or blundering or wayfinding, but luck plays a part in how our stories unfold. How could it not?

Let's put one scenario this way: You go to graduate school with very little concept of what you're interested in. You write an essay on a subject that you also know next to nothing about. Your professor enters it into a contest without telling you, and it wins. You get invited to an international conference with giants in the field. This experience brings you important connections and continues to spark your curiosity. You become a prestigious professor teaching a subject you love, and the rest is history.

You did the work. You knew next to nothing, but your curiosity turned into motivation, which you pursued. You did so well you now teach it. There was luck and hard work. There were many different points where the story could have gone sideways. You might not have entered the right class in the first place. You might have chosen a different curiosity, which didn't lead to opportunities. The most obvious one is that your professor might have seen a good essay and given it an A, but certainly not submitted the essay on your behalf, and so forth.

I actually had a similar situation in which I wrote an essay trying to argue rationally for the existence of God. I had a professor submit it to the Acton Institute. They liked it and offered me a free scholarship to join them at a conference. I was given their course materials and attended workshops and panel discussions. There were opportunities to pursue, but I didn't subscribe to their worldview. I had no interest in pursuing their agenda further. I did learn about myself and what I valued (and didn't) through the process, but it didn't bring about a grand and fulfilling series of career opportunities either.

In the final analysis, because it is so hard to observe ourselves, we must rely on the observations of others. Jack Nicklaus famously said, "The more I practice, the luckier I get." Certainly being willing to try things and "fail fast" as they say, does lead to increased chances of finding your desire. Realizing that luck does play a role can help you have more perspective and modesty about your accomplishments when they come. At the same time, it can help you have compassion for yourself when your initial early dreams don't manifest the way you thought they would when you started out.

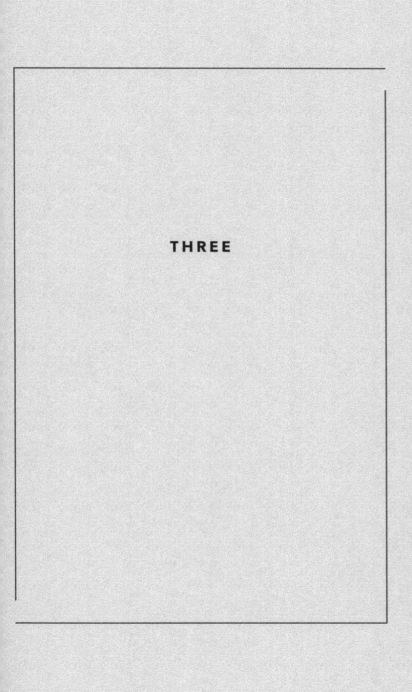

THREE

Time and money

There are 168 hours in a week. If you sleep the normal amount needed for healthy functioning of eight hours a night, that's 56 hours, or nearly one-third of your total time. If you work five days a week from 9-5, you are already up to nearly 100 of your hours and you haven't commuted, showered, eaten, or spent any time with anyone other than presumably your colleagues. Not only are those 40 hours a lot of time in aggregate (and it's unlikely those hours are all actually spent working), you are likely spending a majority of your "premium" time working at your job. Of course, this is great if you love your job, but if you don't, and most people don't, then you are selling your "premium" hours for your salary or hourly wage.

According to Gallup's annual survey of the American Work-force in 2017, 70 percent of employees in the United States are disengaged at work. This number has remained rela-tively unchanged since Gallup began systematically studying employee engagement in 2000. Most people are just getting by, resigning themselves to a job they don't like and spending the premium hours of their years and lives doing work they feel obligated to do.

There are two costs in everything you do. The first is the actual cost in money of an item, activity, or event. The second is less tangible, but more critical, the effective cost of your time. You are constantly making choices which values the use of your time. Choosing to read this book, and how much you will engage with the processes it suggests, for instance.

In "Advice to a Young Tradesman," Benjamin Franklin wrote: "Remember that time is money. He that can earn ten shillings a day by his labour, and goes abroad, or sits idle one half of that day, though he spends but sixpence during his diversion or idleness, it ought not to be reckoned the only expense; he hath really spent or thrown away five shillings besides."

Franklin is saying that if you earn 10 shillings per day, spending half the day doing something aside from work is basically throwing away five shillings. More important is that he's quantifying the value of your time outside of work.

Every decision is the result of a mental calculus, of comparing the implicit costs, or "opportunity costs," and the price tag. Whatever seems to have the most relative value generally wins.

Time gets more valuable as we get older because it has the appearance of moving faster, and we have less and less of it as each day passes. Time seems to move slower when we are experiencing new things.

But while time becomes more valuable as we get older, unfortunately, it doesn't often align with other values (recall our values list at the end of the first chapter). In the corporate world your compensation is based on how much experience you have and how valuable you are to the company, not how valuable your time is to you. You are paid based on your literal market value.

The market doesn't care about you. If you don't value your own time, no one else will.

If money were really so fulfilling why do many multimillionaires and billionaires keep amassing so much wealth? If you have a ballpark of 20 years left in your "life tank" and bank accounts stuffed with funds to last many lifetimes, why are you still spending your time focused on making more money?

Why does nearly everyone feel they don't have enough money? How much money do you really need to bring about the life experiences that will fulfill you? If money is a value, then what are the required principles and behaviors to make money happen?

Does money help or get in the way of your desire?

What would you rather have more of, time or money? Is that a real or false choice? Do you have to choose?

At the end of your life, what will you remember?

Hospice workers around the globe will tell you what they hear. The narratives are similar.

"I wish I'd had the courage to live a life true to myself, not the life others expected of me."

"I wish I hadn't worked so hard."

"I wish I had let myself be happier."

Most of her patients never accomplished even half their dreams, often because they kept working at their "obligations" instead of their desires. Make your desires work for you. You die either way.

Finding and failing with aspirational goals

To this point, we have briefly recognized that we do work within limitations. We want to make sure that we are not sending the misguided and often privileged position of the so-called law of attraction myth. Before we address the concept of manifesting your desires within the scope of prescribed roles that others put on us, let us first make sure we make it clear why desire is so powerful.

On the road to fulfillment, we are faced with choice after choice and not all the choices are well-marked. People talk about listing goals, but those tend to feel overwhelming. Besides, there has been a litany of recent research that demonstrates our goals are only as effective as the processes we put in place to achieve them.

If the primary objective of pursuing desire is to feel good, you can't feel burdened and stressed by the big ambitious goals you set for yourself. Think of goals as giving you a vision toward where you want to be, but don't give yourself hard deadlines. Not yet. Be aspirational at first. The idea is to get to clarity, something I didn't have in my early 20s when I was earnestly searching for what I was supposed to do with my life.

What you do want is direction. Having an idea of where you want to head gives you clarity, which gives you peace of mind. First, feeling calmer makes you all the more likely to experience joy on a regular basis even when you grind to achieve your goals. Second, it feels good to take small, consistent steps toward your goal.

And when you start wearing down from time to time — as you inevitably will no matter how accurate your goals and how well-integrated your values — reach out to others. Your peers will encourage you, give you perspective, remind you why you are important and enough already.

But stick toward your signpost and you will change. Believe it. Feel it.

Taking small steps toward a much larger goal helps you follow your curiosity, try things out, and fail fast. Not "fail fast" in the macho-minded, startup platitude rhetoric. But in the real world way. You are designing your life. Follow broad interests in specific ways. Try stuff out.

I conduct tests all the time. Ever since I left the house on my 18th birthday, I began to stumble upon self discoveries. I had never cooked even once to my recollection at home. Cooking was just something Mom did. But I was hungry a lot in college and the cafeteria wasn't always open. Over the ensuing years, I found I could get by without a cafeteria by cooking, and save money. Over the years I got better and better at cooking. I enjoyed it. But so what? Did that mean it would be my desire to become a chef or start a restaurant? I set out to find out.

For brief periods, I worked in restaurants. I met people, learned from people in our communities, read books, watched documentaries about chefs. I learned as much as I could about the challenges, joys, and travails of owning a small business.

My experiences are not unusual. The point is there are many ways to funnel your learning when you know — and therefore even obliquely pursue — your curiosity about your desire. Opening a restaurant or becoming a chef is not for me.

A few years ago, I knew I liked all kinds of beer. I also like making things from scratch like fresh bread, homemade pasta, roasting my own coffee beans. So, under lots of instruction and encouragement from my brother who had already been brewing for years, I also started brewing my own beer. At first, I didn't know why. I was curious and my brother could expedite my exploration.

Over time, through successes and failures, I got more and more serious. My brother and I started to make weekly batches, documenting the process with spreadsheets and videos, getting better and better equipment, trying different storage styles, different approaches to bottling and kegging. In the process, we learned how ciders were relatively easy to make. We dreamed of what it would entail to own some small rural orchard and open our own cidery or brewery.

But for as fun as it was as a hobby, the idea of turning it into a lifestyle and a business began to feel daunting. It's a high competition and low margin business. It takes hardcore, boots-on-the-ground work daily combined with incredibly precise scientific recipes with expensive equipment.

By the time I realized I didn't want it to become a business, I then had to decide if it was worth the continued investment of time and energy and loads and loads of beer that we ended up mostly giving away. It was a grand experiment, but one I was willing to walk away from with a minimum of investment to learn a lot and have some fun experiments for a couple of years along the way.

I will say that not having a heavy goal kept the process a lot more joyful. I had a vague goal of exploring whether or not I wanted to get into the brewing business while having a good time drinking the results and sharing along the way. Goals like this keep your attention directed. You know how you are spending your Saturdays. You know where that little bit of extra money is going. You know what to order and when you need supplies.

Aspirational goals impact your persistence. They prolong your effort, and they will supply you with more information than you would have had otherwise.

No doubt, goals that are too open-ended go nowhere and usually just fade away. But isn't that better than living less joyously under the oppression of rigid goals? Soldiering on to meet hardcore goals just to prove how tough and amazing you are becomes joyless.

You are not your goals. You are in charge of your life. You are in charge of your joy.

Finding my own desire

This book is about you, but you might want to know more than about my detours. From about the age of ten, I was interested in the possibility of being a writer. I was always fascinated by the experience of a few well-constructed lines having the power to move me on an emotional or intellectual level. I dabbled with writing poems in high school, but the desire to write poems took years to fully discover and embrace.

I took creative writing courses as an undergraduate and during seminary, but it wasn't until after I'd graduated that I began an intentional discovery to read other poets. I was casting about, trying to figure out what I really wanted to do next while paying the bills as a substitute teacher in Naperville, Illinois. I was taking blues guitar lessons, playing pick-up basketball with my roommates and their friends, and checking out books of poetry from the public library by the armload. I wrote almost daily.

I had always read fiction and nonfiction, but not much poetry until my early twenties. Yes, I'm an English major and did read a great deal of Shakespeare and the Romantics and such, but that's not the same. When I began discovering contemporary poets and reading them with my full attention, my growth accelerated.

Poetry is a desire that is almost by definition not going to be a standalone profession, and yet it is also the kind of desire you can pursue all the days of your life. But I had to ask myself, was it going to be like playing guitar and recording a few tunes on my Tascam 4-track? How far was I willing and ready to take my pursuit?

I decided to see if I could specialize in it, become a professor, and make a living at it that way. I studied at Georgia State, started a literary magazine in Atlanta, published in all the literary journals that would take me, and published the poems of others. Eventually, I did become a professor.

For many, at the right institution, teaching the right material under the right conditions, that is as good as it gets. Desire meets identity meets vocation.

After ten years of teaching lots of poetry, fiction, nonfiction, and literature — but mostly freshman composition and research — I followed my desire out the door. My desire was to write, not teach reluctant students how to put a comma in front of a conjunction between two independent clauses.

But how to make a living at writing, and still keep it as my desire?

I tried literary novels; I tried running a nonprofit press; I tried editing; I dabbled in freelancing. Nothing was coming close to making ends meet, and I wasn't particularly fulfilled with the labor either. I kept asking myself: What would be fun and challenging and also meet the criteria of making money? If it wasn't going to be poetry or novels or teaching, what was it?

One day, I stumbled upon my old collection of Choose-Your-Own-Adventures. I remember how much I loved them as a school kid. I did some Google searches, and couldn't believe that there had never been a serious follow up. There was no second generation of interactive fiction. All the talent seemed to have gone to video game design, of which there was a growing trend of games offering multiple narratives through moral-based choices like *The Walking Dead*, *Dishonored*, *Witcher 3*, *Fallout 4*, and many others. I grew fascinated by the endless possibilities of choice-based fiction. I read book after book on game theory. I had found my desire again.

We didn't have much money to put to the new company, but we figured it didn't matter. Our tenacity, and the sheer dynamism of the idea — the storytelling and illustrations — would stand out on their own. We published the first three without promotion or a strategy we could agree on. The e-books became a nightmare to make. You had to learn to code to make sure the reader could land at the exact right spot after making a choice. The books didn't sell, and I had seven others written and partially-illustrated when we ran out of money. It took the better part of a year to come to the painful realization that the project was doomed.

Halfway through that failure, I went from freelancing on parenting and technology to writing supply chain journalism for a freight-tech startup in town. My desire was lost. I was finally making a living as a writer, though, and there was some satisfaction in it. It was exciting to work for a young, ambitious startup, and I stumbled into podcasting and even broadcasting as a host on SiriusXM. The subject matter wasn't my passion, but I was learning. I was growing, and for a time that sustained me.

The startup experience lasted a little over two years before I realized I was burning out. I had learned a lot, even a lot I hadn't expected to learn, but I had lost track of my desire. It was time to take the biggest leap of faith yet, to start the Big Self School with my wife, Shelley.

Keeping up with your desire keeps you alive. It keeps you busy. It leads you into things you might have to learn the hard way, and it leads you into things you didn't know you needed — or wanted — to know.

It's taken the better part of three decades, but I feel like I've arrived at a cross-section of strengths, desire, and experience all merging together. The work is only just beginning, but I think it's safe to say, we've never been happier.

How desire dovetails with vocation

We do well to follow our desire, but there is a reason why it is hard. Few of us have the option to follow our desire outside the confines of how it ties into our vocation. For some elite few with boundless resources, you may decide you want to follow your desire by living on a beach in Costa Rica as a bon vivant. Others choose to "opt out" of prescribed roles and follow desire by living a monastic or artistic life.

The vast majority of us, however, even with other "opt out" options available to us, will choose some kind of engagement within the context of the social and cultural orders that surround us. Our unique freedom to forge an identity all our own based upon desire is constrained. We choose among a menu of roles. We ourselves did not create the roles. The roles set before us were created through inherited historical processes.

This is especially true when it comes to work. It isn't as if all jobs are equally prepared to provide fulfillment, and all we have to do is puzzle piece the best fit based upon our desires. While it is true that our jobs make us who we are every bit as much as who we are leads us to our jobs, it is not always true that our desire has to be found within our jobs. Also, the freedom of our choice to pursue our desire (insofar as it relates to a voca-

tion) must also be weighed with the idea of equal opportunity. Some vocations are incredibly hard for reasons such as a
particular kind of intelligence and the necessary perseverance
to see the training through. Others offer only a small band of
opportunities for similarly skilled applicants. Still, others are
the kind of jobs that are looked down on due to some lack of
comparative prestige. Racial biases persist as well.

This is where we must draw a distinction between desire and
meaning (or purpose). Seeking meaning in life is an end goal
to your self-knowledge work. Following your desire, in our
view, is a means of discovering a direction in which you will
more likely find meaning and purpose. We discuss purpose
and what it means to make an impact in the lives of others in
a separate book. With that said, it is possible that by pursuing
your desire, you are led directly to your purpose.

It really is a matter of emphasis, and this book emphasizes
tuning in to your innermost feelings as guides to what will
give you greater joy, which in turn, step by step, can lead to
a fulfilled life with greater meaning and free from hypocritical
contradictions.

From desire to fulfillment

Pursuing your desire leads to a more joyful, well-lived life, that is more likely to have consistent feelings of fulfillment. What is fulfillment? Our definition:

Satisfaction as a result of integrating your abilities and character in service to a project or cause larger than yourself.

Each day you choose. It's hard to find your desire by choosing what is ordinary, by not building your courage muscle, by allowing money to use up your premium time. Have you ever settled for something much less than you know you want or deserve? It hurts. That's the kind of ache that can leave you reeling — and the same kind that can drive you to reach for something beyond your comfort zone.

Just as you can dictate the terms of your relationship to time and money, you should keep in mind that you are still writing your story. The story you tell yourself isn't set in stone. Do you really know who you are? Are there stories you tell yourself that you say are "just realistic," but that may have kept you down?

Speaking of how others can help us to become the person we dream to be, sometimes they also get in the way. If you're ready to grow, and they are not, you may have to do some re-evaluating. You may need to leave some relationships behind. It's threatening to others when you're ready to take some leaps and follow your desire and they are choosing otherwise.

Fulfillment is possible when you are filling up your cup, honoring your own potential, not forsaking yourself by putting everyone else in front of you. Fulfillment comes when you take bold actions that say "yes" to the future vision of you, even well before your vision is fully realized. Saying "yes" begins forming the future right now.

The process never ends

Following and finding your desire is really about asking yourself, "How's it going?" It's a way of staying in tune.

There is a point where you say, "I'm all done growing and my life is great." You know when that is? When it's time for someone to write your eulogy.

How do you want your eulogy to go?

She had everything she could want and she could really relax on the beach.

You might be able to create that reality. Those of us having to maintain our 9-to-5 might be forming a life more like:

He had great analytical skills and kept a balanced spreadsheet.

She knew how to hire and fire and manage shifting priorities and difficult personalities.

You probably want more than a few attributes on a job posting. If you're reading this it's likely enough that your life is pretty okay in a number of respects. Maybe it's clear that you're missing a vague something, or maybe a crisis or transition has alerted you to something clear you've missed and now need to prioritize.

The question isn't just how do you want to feel. The question now becomes: What do I need to do to get there? You may need to consider the negative feelings that are in your way. Is there a past failure that you can't let go, and that you're beating yourself up over? If you need to heal, what process have you been ignoring that will help you do just that? Is your inner critic chastising you? What obstacles must you deal with in order to move forward?

Working through the negative gets you to the positive. What are your best successes? How did you make them happen? How did they (or do they) make you feel? How do you create similar conditions to making a new success happen? Who supports you the most? Who has proven it can be done?

These are the tune-up questions that lead you forward to your desire. Life is a never-ending pursuit of your building. If that sounds exhausting, don't worry, part of living a joy-filled life is taking restorative breaks. You find joy by pursuing your desire, and you find desire by breaking open the static cling of the past, by refusing bland and repetitive roles and bending to others' ideas for what you should do. You access the deep inner longing by wayfinding, through trial and error, big dreams made with tiny steps, and loads of self-compassion.

And, seriously, what else would you rather be doing?

THE BIG SELF SCHOOL

The Big Self School is a personal growth learning community, whose central mission is to help you deepen your self-knowledge so that you can improve your life. We create digital courses, online community, books, and media designed to activate self-awareness, deeper connections, bold action, and healthy habits so you can play big without burning out.

www.bigselfschool.com

ABOUT THE AUTHOR

Chad Prevost has advanced degrees in creative writing, literature, and theology. A workshop leader and entrepreneur, he has started and participated in writing and literary arts communities in Atlanta, Austin, Chattanooga, and New York. He also has experience writing as a journalist for startups in tech and logistics. He is the author of several books of poetry, as well as interactive-fiction for young adults. He has innovated writing processes to foster reflection and insight, narrative strength, and authentic voice since 2004. Chad supports the Oxford Comma.